The Green Pamphlet

The Grievances of the British Indians in South Africa: An Appeal to the Indian Public

By Mohandas K. Gandhi

RAJKOT, KATHIAWAR

Dated at Durban, Natal, this 26th day of May 1896.

We, the undersigned, representing the Indian community in South Africa, hereby appoint M. K. Gandhi, Esq., of Durban, Advocate, to represent the grievances the Indians are labouring under in South Africa before the authorities and public men and public bodies in India.

ABDOOL CARIM HAJI ADAM (DADA ABDOOLLA & CO.)

ABDUL CADER (MAHOMED CASSIM CAMROODEEN)

P. DAWAJEE MAHOMED

HOOSEN CASSIM

A. C. PILLAY

PARSEE RUSTOMJI

A. M. TILLY

HAJEE MAHOMED H. DADA

AMOD MAHOMED PARUK

ADAMJI MIANKHAN

PEERUN MAHOMED

A. M. SALOOJEE

DOWD MAHOMED

AMOD JEEWA HOOSEN MEERUM

K. S. PILLAY & CO.

AHMEDJI DOWJI MOGRARIA

MOOSA HAJEE CASSIM

G. A. BASSA

MANILAL CHATURBHAI

M. E. KATHRADA

D. M. TIMOL

DAVJEE M. SEEDAT

ISMAIL TIMOL

SHAIK FAREED & CO.

SHAIKHJEE AMOD

MAHOMED CASSIM HAFFIJI

AMOD HOOSEN

MAHOMED AMOD BASSA

V. A. ESSOP

MAHOMED SULEMAN

DAWJEE MAMAD MUTALA

SULEMAN VORAJI

EBRAHIM NOOR MAHOMED

MAHOMED SULEMAN KHOTA

CHOOHURMAL LUCHERAM

NARAYAN PATHER

VIJAYA RAGAVALOO

SULIMAN DAWJEE

The Grievances of the British Indians in South Africa: An Appeal to the Indian Public (14-8-1896)

August 14, 1896

This is an appeal to the Indian public on behalf of the 100,000 Indians in South Africa. I have been commissioned by the leading members representing that community in South Africa to lay before the public in India the grievances that her Majesty's Indian subjects are labouring under in that country.

South Africa is a continent by itself and is divided into many States of which the Colonies of Natal and the Cape of Good Hope, Zululand, a Crown Colony, the South African Republic of the Transvaal, Orange Free State and the Chartered Territories, are inhabited, more or less, by the Indians together with the Europeans and the natives of those countries. The Portuguese territories, viz., Delagoa Bay, Beira and Mozambique, have a large Indian population, but there the Indians have no grievances, apart from the general population.

NATAL

From an Indian standpoint, Natal is the most important portion of South Africa. It has a native population of about 400,000, a European population of nearly 50,000 and an Indian population of about 51,000, of whom about 16,000 are those at present serving their indenture, about 30,000 are those who, having once been under indenture, are freed therefrom and have settled in the Colony on their own account, and about 5,000 belong to the trading community.

These latter, of course, came to the Colony on their own means and some of them brought capital also into the country. The indentured Indians are drawn from the labouring population of Madras and Calcutta and are nearly equally divided. Those from Madras speak, as a rule, the Tamil language, and those from Calcutta, the Hindi. Most of them are Hindus, a good few are Mahomedans. Strictly speaking, they do not observe caste restrictions. After becoming free, they either take to gardening or hawking vegetables and earn from 2 to 3 pounds sterling per month. A few become petty storekeepers. That business, however, is practically in the hands of the 5,000 Indians, who are drawn chiefly from the Mahomedan community in the Bombay Presidency. Some of these latter are doing well. Many are large landowners, two are now shipowners also. One of them has a small oil machine worked by steam. They come either from Surat, or districts surrounding Bombay, or Porbandar. Many merchants from Surat have settled in Durban with their families. Most of them, including the assisted immigrants, can read and write their own language to a greater extent than one would think they do.

I venture to quote the following from my 'Open Letter' to the Members of the Legislative Assembly and the Legislative Council of Natal to show what treatment the Indian receives at the hands of the general run of Europeans in the Colony:

"The man in the street hates him, curses him, spits upon him, and often pushes him off the foot-path. The Press cannot find a sufficiently strong word in the best English dictionary to damn him with. Here are a few samples. "The real canker that is eating into the very vitals of the community", "these parasites", "wily, wretched semi-barbarous Asiatics", "A thing black and lean and a long way from clean, which they call the accursed Hindoo", "He is chock-full of vice and he lives upon rice. I heartily cuss the Hindoo", "Squalid coolies with truthless tongues and artful ways". The Press almost unanimously refuses to call the Indian by his proper name. He is "Ramysamy". He is "Mr. Samy". He is "Mr. Coolie". He is "the black man". And these offensive epithets have become so common that they (at any rate, one of them, "Coolie") are used even in the sacred precincts of the courts, as if "the Coolie" were the legal and proper name to give to any and every Indian. The public men, too, seem to use the word freely. I have often heard the painful expression "coolie clerk" from the mouths of men who ought to know better. The tramcars are not for the Indians. The railway officials may treat the Indians as beasts, No matter how clean, his very sight is such an offence to every White man in the Colony that he would object to sit, even for a short time, in the same compartment with the Indian. The hotels shut their doors against them. Even the public baths are not for the Indians no matter who they are... The vagrant law is needlessly oppressive and often puts respectable Indians in a very awkward position."

?

I have quoted this because the statement has been before the South African public for nearly one year and a half, has been commented upon freely by almost every newspaper in South Africa and remains practically uncontradicted (indeed, it has even been endorsed by one newspaper with approval) and because, during the interval that has elapsed, I have seen nothing to change that view. The Right Honourable Mr. Chamberlain, however, while in full sympathy with its object, in his reply to the deputation headed by the Hon'ble Mr. Dadabhai is said to have stated that our grievances were more sentimental than material and real and that, if he could be shown any instances of real grievance, he should deal with them effectively. The Times of India, which has done us much service and has laid us under deep obligation to it by its persistent advocacy on our behalf, rebuked Mr. Chamberlain for calling our grievances sentimental. To give, however, proof of real grievances and to strengthen the position of the advocates of our cause in India, I shall beg leave to cite my own testimony and that of those who have undergone grievances personally. Every word of every statement to be made immediately can be established beyond the shadow of a doubt.

In Dundee last year, during the Christmas time, a gang of White men set fire to the Indian stores without the slightest provocation, in order to enjoy themselves. Mr. Abdulla Haji Adam, a shipowner and one of the leading members of the Indian community in South Africa, was travelling with me as far as Krantzkloof Station. He alighted there to go by postal cart to Natal. No one there would sell him even bread. The hotelkeeper would not allow him a room in his hotel and he had to sleep in the coach, shivering the whole night with cold. And the winter in that part of Africa is no joke. Mr. Haji Mohamed Haji Dada, another leading Indian gentleman, was travelling in a coach some time ago from Pretoria to Charlestown. He was forced out of the coach and had to walk a distance of three miles because he had not got a pass-- whatever that may mean.

A Parsee gentleman, Mr. Rustomjee, whose generosity goes much further than his purse would allow, has been unable to take a Turkish bath for the sake of his health in Durban, although the public baths are the property of the Durban Corporation, to which Mr. Rustomjee pays his rates just as well as the other ratepayers. In Field Street, Durban, last year during Christmas time, some youths threw burning crackers in the Indian stores doing some damage. Three months ago, in the same street, some youths shot lead bullets into an Indian store with a sling, hurting a customer who nearly lost his eye. Both these matters were brought to the notice of the Superintendent of Police who promised to do all he could. Nothing more has been heard of the matter. Yet the Superintendent is an estimable gentleman, anxious to protect all the communities in Durban. But what could the poor man do against the tremendous odds? Will his subordinates take the trouble to find out the miscreants? When the aggrieved gentleman saw the constables at the police station, they first laughed and then asked him to get a warrant from the Magistrate for their arrest. No warrant is required in such cases when a constable wants to do his duty. Only the day before I left Natal, the son of an Indian gentleman, spotlessly dressed, was walking along the pavement in the principal street in Durban. Some Europeans pushed him off the pavement without any reason but to amuse themselves. Last year, the Magistrate at Estcourt, a village in Natal, had an Indian who was a prisoner in the dock forced out of it. His cap was forcibly removed and he was brought back bare-headed, in spite of the protest from the man that the removal of the cap was contrary to Indian custom and it offended his religious feeling also. A civil action was brought against the Magistrate. And the judges held that the Magistrate was not civilly liable for acts done by him in his capacity as such. When we went to law, we knew that such would be the decision. Our object was to have the matter thoroughly thrashed out. This question at one time was a very great question in the colony.

An Indian official, whenever he accompanies his superior during his periodical tours, is unable to secure accommodation in the hotels. He is obliged to sojourn in huts. The grievance had reached such a stage, when I left Natal, that he was seriously thinking of sending in his resignation.

A Eurasian gentleman, Mr. DeSilva by name, who was for some time employed in a responsible position in Fiji, happened to come to Natal to seek fortune. He is a certified chemist. He received an appointment as chemist by letter. When, however, his employer saw that he was not quite White, he dismissed him. I know other Eurasians who, being fair enough to pass as "White men", are not molested. This last instance I have quoted to show how unreasonable the prejudice is in Natal. I could go on relating such instances. But, I hope, I have adduced sufficient instances to show that our grievances are real and as one of our sympathizers in England says in a letter, "They have only to be known to be removed."

Now, what is our mode of action in such cases? Are we to go to Mr. Chamberlain in every case and turn the Colonial Office into one for hearing petty complaints from Indians in South Africa? I have used the word "petty" advisedly, for I admit that most of these cases are cases of petty assault and inconvenience. But when they occur pretty regularly, they assume a sufficiently big shape to be a source of constant irritation to us. Just picture a country where you never know you are safe from such assaults, no matter who you are, where you have a nervous fear as to what would happen to you whenever you undertake a journey, where you cannot be accommodated in a hotel even for a night and you have a picture of the state we are living in Natal. I am sure I am not exaggerating when I say that, if any of the Indian High Court Judges came to South Africa, I doubt very much whether any hotel would admit him, unless he took extraordinary precautions, and I am almost positive that he will have to travel from Charlestown to Pretoria in a Kaffir compartment, unless he is dressed in European clothing from top to toe.

I am aware that in some of the instances cited above Mr. Chamberlain could not very well afford relief, as for example the case of Mr. DeSilva, but the fact is clear that such instances occur because of the rooted prejudice against the Indians in South Africa, which is due to the indifference of the Home and the Indian Governments to the complaints of the Indians. In all the cases of assault, our mode of action, as a rule, is not to take any notice of them. We follow the principle, so far as we can, of going two miles when we are asked to go one. Sufferance is, really and sincerely, the badge of the Indians in South Africa, especially in Natal. I may state, however, that we follow this policy not from philanthropic but from purely selfish motives. We have found by painful experiences that to bring the offenders to justice is a tedious and expensive process. The result is often contrary to our expectations. The offender would either be discharged with a caution or fined "five shillings or one day". The very man, after getting out of the box, assumes a more threatening attitude and puts the complainant in an awkward position. And the publication of such acts incites others to similar ones. We, therefore, do not, as a rule, even mention them before the public in Natal.

Such a feeling of deep-seated hatred towards the Indians is reproduced all over South Africa, in special legislation for Indians, which has for its object the degradation of the Indian community in that country. The Attorney-General of Natal wants to keep the Indians for ever "hewers of wood and drawers of water". We are classed with the natives of South Africa-Kaffir race. He defines the status of the Indians in the following words: "These Indians were brought here for the purpose of supplying labour for development of local industries and were not intended to form portion of the South African nation which was being built up in the various States." The policy of the Orange Free State, which, in the words of its leading organ, "has made the British Indian an impossibility by simply classifying him with the South African natives", is cherished by the other States as a model policy. What that State has completely accomplished, the other States would accomplish within a very short time but for the vigilance of the Indian public. We are passing through a crisis now. We are hemmed in on all sides by restrictions and high-handed measures.

I shall now show how the feeling of hatred above described has been crystallized into legislation. An Indian cannot leave his house after 9 o'clock at night unless he has a pass signed by someone showing that he is out under instructions or can give a good account of himself. This law applies to the natives and Indians only. The police use their discretion and do not, as a rule, trouble those who are dressed in the Memon costume, as that dress is supposed to be the Indian trader's dress. Mr. Aboobaker, now deceased, was the foremost Indian trader in Natal and much respected by the European community. He, with his friend, was once arrested by the police. When he was brought to the police station for being out after 9 p. m., the authorities knew at once that they had committed a mistake. They told Mr. Aboobaker that they did not want to arrest gentlemen like himself, and asked him if he could point out any distinguishing mark between a trader and a labourer. Mr. Aboobaker pointed to his robe, and, ever since, it has been a tacit understanding between the police and the public that those wearing the flowing robe should not be arrested, even though they may be out after 9

p.m. But there are Tamil and Bengali traders, equally respectable, who do not wear the robes. There are, again, the Christian Indian educated youths-a most sensitive class-who do not wear robes. They are constantly molested. A young Indian, well educated and a Sunday school teacher, another a schoolmaster, were arrested only four months ago and locked up in a dungeon the whole night, in spite of their protestations that they were on their way home. They were discharged by the Magistrate but that was a poor consolation. An Indian lady, a teacher, the wife of the Indian Interpreter at Ladysmith, was a short time ago on her return from the church on a Sunday evening, arrested by two Kaffir policemen and roughly handled, so much so that her dress was soiled, not to speak of all sorts of bad names she was called. She was locked up in a cell. She was promptly released when the Superintendent of Police came to know who she was. She was carried home senseless. The bold lady sued the Corporation for damages for wrongful arrest and got ?0 and costs from the Supreme Court. The Chief Justice remarked that her treatment was "unjust, harsh, arbitrary and tyrannical". The result, however, of these three cases is that the Corporations are now clamouring for more powers and an alteration of the law, in order that they may, to put it bluntly, subject all Indians, irrespective of their position, to restrictions so that, as a member of the Legislative Assembly said on the occasion of the passing of the Immigration Bill of 1894, "the intention of the Colony to make the Indian's life more comfortable in his native land than in the Colony of Natal" may be fulfilled. In any other country, such instances would have excited the sympathy of all right-minded people and the decision quoted above would have been hailed with joy.

Some eight months ago, about 20 Indians, pure labourers on their way to the Durban market with vegetable baskets on their heads, a sufficient indication that they were not vagrants, were arrested at 4 o'clock in the morning under the same law. The police prosecuted the case vigorously. After a two days' trial, the Magistrate discharged them, but at what cost to the poor people! They were carrying their day's earnings in prospect on their shoulders. These were gone. They were, I believe, detained for two days in gaol and had to pay their attorney's fees in the bargain, for having ventured to be up and doing in the early morning, a fitting reward for industry! And Mr. Chamberlain wants instances of real grievances!

There is a system of passes in Natal. Any Indian who, whether in the day-time or the night-time, does not show a pass as to who he is, is liable to arrest. This is meant to prevent desertion by the indentured Indians and to facilitate identification and is thus far, I believe, necessary, but the working of the law is extremely irritating and a crying grievance. But for the cruel feeling, no injustice need occur under that law. Let the papers speak for themselves as to the working of the law. The Natal Advertiser of the 19th June, 1895, has the following on the subject:

"I wish to bring before your notice a few facts regarding the manner in which the Cato Manor tenants are arrested under section 31, Law 25 of 1891. When they are walking on their grounds, the policemen come and arrest them and ask for their free passes. When they call out for their wives or relatives to produce the passes, before they can be produced the policemen begin to drag the Indians to the police-station. When the passes are produced on the road to the station, the policemen simply look at them and throw them to the ground. The Indians are taken to the police-station, detained for a night and made to wash the cell out in the morning and are then brought before the Magistrate. The Magistrate, without taking their pleas, fines them. When they reported this to the Protector, he told them to go to the Magistrate, yet (adds the correspondent) he is appointed to protect the Indian immigrants. If such things exist in the Colony (continues the writer), to whom are they to appeal?"

?

The statement that the Magistrate does not take pleas must, I think, be a mistake.

The Natal Mercury, the Government organ in Natal, of 13th April, 1895, has the following from the Editor:

"A point of considerable importance to respectable Indians and which causes much heart-burning, is their liability to arrest. Let me give a case in point. A well-known Durban Indian who has property in various parts of the town, a well-educated and exceedingly intelligent man, was the other night, with his mother, visiting Sydenham, where also he has property. Met by two native constables, the young man and his mother were taken into custody and marched off to the police-station, though it is only fair to say the native police conducted themselves admirably. The young Indian referred to explained who he was and gave references and the trooper at length bade him begone, warning him, however, that if he did not have a pass next time he would be detained and prosecuted. Being a British subject in a British Colony, he objects to being treated in this way, though, of course, he recognizes the necessity of watchfulness in general. He makes a very strong point, however, and one which the authorities should certainly consider."

?

It will be only fair to state what the authorities have to say. They admit the grievance but ask how they are to distinguish between an indentured Indian and a free Indian. We, on the other hand, submit that nothing can be easier. The indentured Indian never is dressed in a fashionable dress. The presumption should be in favour of, not against, the Indian, especially an Indian of the type I am referring to. There is no more reason to presume a man to be a thief than to presume an Indian to be a deserter. Even if an Indian did desert and made preparations to look decent, it will be difficult for him to remain undetected for a long time. But, then, the Indian in South Africa is not credited with any feelings. He is a beast, "a thing black and lean", "the Asian dirt to be heartily cursed".

There is, again, a law which says that natives and Indians, when driving cattle, must be provided with certain passes; also a bye-law in Durban which provides for the registration of native servants and "others belonging to the uncivilized races of Asia". This presupposes that the Indian is a barbarian. There is a very good reason for requiring registration of a native in that he is yet being taught the dignity and necessity of labour. The Indian knows it and he is imported because he knows it. Yet, to have the pleasure of classifying him with the natives, he too is required to be registered. The Superintendent of the Borough Police has never, so far as I know, put the law in motion. Once I raised an objection, in defending an Indian servant, that he was not registered. The Superintendent resented the objection and said he never applied the law to Indians and asked me if I wanted to see them degraded. The law, however, being there, may at any time be used as an engine of oppression.

But we have not attempted to have any of these disabilities removed. We are doing what we can to have their rigour mitigated locally. For the present, our efforts are concentrated towards preventing and getting repealed fresh legislation. Before referring to that, I may further illustrate the proposition that the Indian is put on the same level with the native in many other ways also. Lavatories are marked "natives and Asiatics" at the railway stations. In the Durban Post and Telegraph Offices, there were separate entrances for natives and Asiatics and Europeans. We felt the indignity too much and many respectable Indians were insulted and called all sorts of names by the clerks at the counter. We petitioned the authorities to do away with the invidious distinction and they have now provided three separate entrances for natives, Asiatics and Europeans.

The Indians have, up to now, enjoyed the franchise rights under the general franchise law of the colony, which requires ownership of immovable property worth ?0 or payment of an annual rental of ?0 to qualify an adult male to be placed on the Voters' Roll. There is a special franchise law for the natives. Under the former, in 1894, there were 9,309 European voters and 251 Indians, of whom only 203 were living at the time, the populations being equal. Thus the European vote in 1894 was 38 times as strong as the Indian vote. Yet, the Government thought or pretended to think that there was a real danger of the Asiatic vote swamping the Europeans. They, therefore, introduced into the Legislative Assembly of Natal a Bill disfranchising all Asiatics save those who were then rightly contained in any Voters' List, the preamble of the Bill stating that the Asiatics were not acquainted with elective representative institutions. Against this Bill we memorialized both the Legislative Assembly and the Legislative Council of Natal but to no purpose. We then memorialized Lord Ripon and forwarded copies of the memorial to the Press and the public in India and England, with a view to enlist their sympathy and to secure their active support which, we are thankful to say, we received to some extent.

As a result, that Act has now been repealed and replaced by an Act which says "no persons shall be qualified to have their names inserted in any list of electors who (not being of European origin) are natives or descendants in the male line of natives of countries which have not hitherto possessed elective representative institutions founded on the parliamentary franchise unless they shall first obtain an order from the Governor-in-Council, exempting them from the operation of the Act." It also exempts from its operation those persons that are rightly contained in any Voters' List. This Bill was first submitted to Mr. Chamberlain who has practically approved of it. We, yet, thought it advisable to oppose it and, with a view to secure its disallowance, have sent a memorial to Mr. Chamberlain and hope to secure the same measure of support that has been extended to us hitherto. We believe that the real reason for all such legislation is to accord a different treatment to the Indian in South Africa, such that, under it, a respectable Indian in that country may become an impossibility. There is no real danger of the Asiatic vote swamping the European or the Asiatic ruling South Africa. Yet this was the main point urged in support of the Bill. The whole question has been well thrashed out in the Colony and Mr. Chamberlain has got all the materials before him to judge. Here are the Government giving their own view in their organ, The Natal Mercury, of the 5th March, 1896, dealing with the present Bill and supporting it. After quoting the figures from the Voters' List it says:

"The fact of the matter is that apart from numbers altogether the superior race will always hold the reins of Government. We are inclined to the belief therefore that the danger of the Indian vote swamping the European is a chimerical one. We do not consider that the danger of being swamped is at all a likely one, as past experience has proved that the class of Indians coming here, as a rule, do not concern themselves about the franchise and further that the majority of them do not even possess the small property qualification required."

This admission has been reluctantly made. The Mercury supposes, and we believe, that the Bill will fail in its purpose if it is to debar the Asiatic from the franchise and says that it would not matter if it does. What, then, is the object if it be not to harass the Indian community? The real reason why the Bill has been introduced is thus guardedly but frankly stated by the Mercury of the 23rd April, 1896:

"Rightly or wrongly, justly or unjustly, a strong feeling exists among the Europeans in South Africa, and especially in the two Republics, against Indians or any other Asiatics being allowed unrestricted right to the franchise."

?

The Indian argument, or course, is that there is only one Indian to every 38 European voters on the Roll at present with the open franchise and that the danger anticipated is imaginary. Perhaps it is, but we have to deal with it as if it were a real danger, not altogether, as we have explained, because of our views, but because of the views we know to be strongly held by the rest of the Europeans in the country. We do not want isolation again under the far greater and more fatal ban of being a semi-Asiatic country out of touch and out of harmony with the other European Governments of the country.

This, then, is the naked truth. In obedience to the popular outcry, justly or unjustly, the Asiatic must be put down. This Bill has been passed after a secret meeting was held by the Government at which they explained the real reasons for passing the Bill. It has been condemned by the Colonists' and the other newspapers as inadequate from their point of view and by the very members who voted for it. They hold that the Bill will not apply to the Indians because they possess in India "elective representative institutions founded on the Parliamentary franchise and that it will involve the Colony in endless litigation and agitation". We, too, have taken up the same ground. We have urged that the Legislative Councils in India are "elective representative institutions founded on the Parliamentary franchise". Of course, in the popular sense of the term, we have no such institutions, but in the opinion of the London Times and an able jurist in Durban our institutions can well be legally classified under those described in the Bill. The Times says "the argument that he (the Indian) has no franchise whatever in India in inconsistent with facts." Mr. Laughton, an eminent lawyer in Natal, writing to a newspaper on the subject, says:

"Is there, then, a Parliamentary (or legislative) franchise in India, and what is it? There is, and it was created by the Acts 24 and 25 Victoria, Chapter 67, and 55 and 56 Victoria, Chapter 140, by the regulations made under Section 4 of the latter Act. It may not be founded on what we call a liberal basis, it may indeed be founded on a very crude basis, but it is the Parliamentary franchise nevertheless and, under the Bill it is on it that elective representative institutions of India have to be founded."

?

This is also the opinion of other eminent men in Natal. Mr. Chamberlain, however, in his despatch in connection with the matter says

"I also recognize the fact that the natives of India do not possess representative institutions in their own country and that they themselves, in those periods of their history when they were exempt from European influence, have never set up any such system themselves."

?

The opinion, as will be noticed, is opposed to the view expressed by The Times partly quoted above and has naturally frightened us. We are anxious to know what the best legal opinion here is. We cannot, however, too often urge that it is not political power that we want but it is the degradation which these Franchise Bills involve that we resist. If a Colony is allowed to treat the Indians on a different footing from the Europeans in one respect, there would be no difficulty in going further. Their goal is not merely disfranchisement. Their goal is total extinction of the Indian. He may be allowed to exist there as a pariah, as an indentured labourer, at the most a free labourer, but he must not aspire higher. At the time the first Franchise Bill was introduced, in response to the clamour for Municipal disfranchisement of the Indians, the Attorney-General said that would be dealt with in the near future. The Natal Government, about a year ago, wished to convene what was called a "Coolie Conference", so that there might be uniformity in Indian legislation throughout South Africa. At that time also, the Deputy Mayor of Durban moved a resolution that the Asiatics should be induced to live in separate locations. The Government are vexing themselves to find out how they can directly and effectively check the influx of the Indian traders, whom Mr. Chamberlain describes to be "peaceable, law-abiding, meritorious body of persons whose undoubted industry and intelligence and indomitable perseverance", he hopes, "will suffice to overcome any obstacles which may now face them in pursuit of their avocations". The present Bill, therefore, we humbly think, has to be taken in connection with these facts and treated accordingly. The London Times has put the franchise question in this form:

"The question now before Mr. Chamberlain is not an academic one. It is not a question of argument but of race feeling. We cannot afford a war of races among our own subjects. It would be as wrong for the Government of India to suddenly arrest the development of Natal by shutting off the supply of immigrants as it would be for Natal to deny the rights of citizenship to British Indian subjects who, by years of thrift and good work in the Colony, have raised themselves to the actual status of citizens."

The Second Bill that has been passed by the Natal Legislature proposes to keep the indentured Indians always under indenture, or if they do not relish it, to send them back to India at the end of the first indenture of five years, or if they would not go back, then to compel them to pay an annual tax of ?3. How, in a British Colony, such a measure could even be thought of passes our comprehension. Almost all the public men in Natal are agreed that the prosperity of the Colony depends upon the Indian labour. In the words of a present member of the Legislative Assembly, "at the time the Indian immigration was decided upon the progress and almost the existence of the Colony hung in the balance!" But in the words of another eminent Natalian,

"Indian immigration brought prosperity, prices rose, people were no longer content to grow or sell produce for a song, they could do better. If we look to 1859, we shall find that the assured promise of Indian labour resulted in an immediate rise of revenue which increased fourfold within a few years. Mechanics who could not get a wage and were earning 5 shillings a day and less found their wages more than doubled and progress gave encouragement to everyone from the Burgh to the Sea."

Yet they want to tax these industrious and indispensable people who, in the words of the present Chief Justice of Natal, have turned out to be "trustworthy and useful domestic servants", after having taken the very life-blood out of them. The following opinion was held by the present Attorney-General ten years ago. He is now the framer of this Bill which a Radical newspaper in London says "is a monstrous wrong, an insult to British subjects, a disgrace to its authors and a slight upon ourselves".

"With reference to the time-expired Indians, I do not think that it ought to be compulsory on any man to go to any part of the world save for a crime for which he is transported. I hear a great deal of this question. I have been asked again and again to take a different view but I have not been able to do it. A man is brought here, in theory with his own consent, in practice very often without. He gives the best five years of his life, he forms new ties, forgets the old ones perhaps, establishes a home here and he cannot, according to my view of right and wrong, be sent back. Better by far to stop the further introduction of Indians altogether than to take what work you can out of them and order them away."

But now that which was meritorious 10 years ago in the Indian, namely, his service to the Colony for 5 years for a paltry wage, has become a crime for which he would deserve transportation to India, if the Natal Attorney-General be allowed to do so by the Indian and the Home Governments. I may mention that the Indian Government, on the representation of an ex parte Commission that visited India from Natal in 1893, have accepted the principle of compulsory indenture. We, however, are hoping confidently that the facts brought out in the memorials to the Home and the Indian Governments are sufficient to induce the latter to alter their views.

Although we have not moved in the matters specially affecting the Indians now serving their indenture, one may well presume that their lot will not be practically comfortable on the estates. We think that the alteration in the Colony's tone with regard to the general population will affect the masters also of the indentured Indians. One or two matters, however, I have been asked to especially bring to the notice of the public. A representation was made, even as far back as 1891, by an Indian Committee headed by Mr. Haji Mohamed Haji Dada, one of the prayers whereof being that the Protector of Immigrants should be a man knowing the Tamil and the Hindustani languages and should, if possible, be an Indian. We have not receded from that position, but the interval has merely confirmed that opinion. The present Protector is an estimable gentleman. His ignorance of the languages, however, cannot but be a serious drawback. We humbly consider also that the protector should be instructed to act as an advocate for the Indian more than as Judge between the employers and the immigrants. I shall illustrate what I say. An Indian named Balasundaram was, in 1894, so ill-treated by his master that two of his teeth were nearly knocked out; they came out through his upper lip causing an issue of blood sufficient to soak his long turban in it. His master admitted the fact but pleaded grave provocation, denied by the man. On receiving the punishment, he seems to have gone to the Protector's house which was close by his master's. The Protector sent word that he must go to his office the next day.

The man went, then, to the Magistrate who was much moved at the sight. The turban was kept in court and he was at once sent to the hospital for treatment. The man after having been kept in the hospital for a few days was discharged. He had heard about me and came to my office. He had not recovered sufficiently to be able to speak. I asked him, therefore, to write out his complaint in Tamil which he knew. He wanted to prosecute the master so that his contract of indenture might be cancelled. I asked him if he would be satisfied if his indenture was transferred. On his nodding consent to what I said, I wrote to his master asking if he would consent to transfer the services of the man. He was at first unwilling but subsequently consented. I sent the man also to the Protector's office with a Tamil clerk of mine who gave the man's version to the Protector. The Protector desired the man to be left in his office and sent word that he would do his best. The master, in the mean while, went to the Protector's office and changed his mind, saying his wife would not agree to the transfer because his services were invaluable. The man was then said to have compromised and to have given the Protector a written document to the effect that he had no complaint to make. He sent me a note to the effect that as the man had no complaint to make and his master did not consent to transfer the services he would not interfere in the matter. I ask if this was right. Was it right for the Protector to have taken such a document from the man? Did he want to protect himself against the man? To proceed, however, with the painful story, naturally the note sent a shock through my body. I had hardly recovered when the man came to my office crying and saying the Protector would not transfer him. I literally ran to the Protector's office and inquired what the matter was. He placed the written document before me and asked me how he could help the man. He said the man should not have signed the document. And this document was an affidavit attested by the Protector himself. I told the Protector that I should advise the man to go to the Magistrate and lodge a complaint. He said the document would be produced before the Magistrate and it would be useless. He advised me, therefore, to drop the matter. I returned to my office and wrote a letter to his master imploring him to consent to the transfer. The master would do nothing of the kind. The magistrate treated us quite differently. He had seen the man while the blood was yet dripping from his lips. The deposition was duly made. On the day of hearing, I explained the whole circumstances and again appealed to the master in open court and offered to withdraw the complaint if he consented to the transfer. The Magistrate then gave the master to understand that, unless he considered my offer more favourably than he seemed to do at the time, consequences might be serious for him. He went on to say that he thought the man was brutally treated. The master said he gave provocation. The Magistrate retorted: "You had no business to take the law in your own hands and beat the man as if he were a beast." He adjourned the case for one day in order to enable the master to consider the offer made by me. The master, of course, came down and consented. The Protector then wrote to me that he would not agree to transfer unless I submitted a European name he could approve of. Happily, the Colony is not quite devoid of benevolent men. A Wesleyan local preacher and solicitor, out of charity, undertook to take over the man's services, and thus ended the last act of this painful drama. Comment is superfluous as to the procedure adopted by the Protector. This is only a typical instance showing how hard it is for the indentured men to get justice.

We submit that no matter who he is, his duties should be clearly defined as are those of judges, advocates, solicitors and others. Certain things, for the sake of avoiding temptations, he should not be able to do in spite of himself. Just fancy a judge being the guest of a criminal who is being tried before him. Yet, the Protector, when he goes to the estates to enquire about the condition of the men and to hear complaints, can and does often become the guest of the employers.

We submit that this practice is wrong in principle, no matter how highminded the Protector may be. As a Surgeon-Superintendent of Immigrants remarked the other day, the Protector should be easily approachable to the meanest coolie, but he should be unapproachable to the lordliest employer. He may not be a Natal man. It also looks a strange procedure to appoint as Protector a member of a Commission whose object is to induce the Indian Government to consent to pass harsher laws for the indentured Indians. When the Protector has to perform such a conflicting duty, who is to protect the indentured men?

It should be easy for the immigrant to have his services transferred. There are in the gaol some Indians who have been there for years because they refuse to go to their employers. They say they have complaints which, owing to the peculiar circumstances in which they are placed, they cannot substantiate. A Magistrate was so much disgusted with the business that he wished he had not to try such cases. The Natal Mercury of 13th June, 1895, thus comments on such a case:

"When a man, even a coolie immigrant, prefers to go to prison rather than work for the master to whom he has been indentured, the natural inference is that something is wrong somewhere, and we are not surprised at Mr. Dillon's remarks on Saturday, when he had three coolies before him, all charged with the same offence of refusing to work, all giving the same excuse, viz., that they were ill-treated by their masters. Of course, it is just possible that these particular coolies prefer gaol work to plantation work. On the other hand, it is just possible that the coolies have some ground for their complaint as to their treatment and the matter is one that ought to be investigated, and at least these men who complain in this way should be transferred to another master and, if they again refuse to work, it can be readily seen that they do not want to work. If a coolie is ill-treated it may be said that he can complain to the Magistrate, but it is not an easy matter for any coolie to prove such cases. It is a matter altogether for the Protector of Immigrants to inquire into and remedy, if possible."

There is an Immigration Trust Board that consists of employers of Indians. They have now received very wide powers. And seeing the position they occupy, their acts will have to be very jealously watched by the Indian Government. The punishment for desertion is heavy enough, and yet they are now seriously considering whether some stiffer mode of dealing with such cases could not be devised. It should be remembered, however, that, in at least 9 cases out of 10, the socalled deserters complain of ill-treatment, and such deserters are protected under the law from punishment, but as the poor fellows cannot establish their complaints, they are treated as real deserters and sent by the Protector to the Magistrate for punishment accordingly. Under such circumstances, any alteration for the worse in the law about desertion should, we submit, require careful consideration.

There is a sad mortality among these people from suicides. They are not satisfactorily accounted for. I cannot do better than quote the Advertiser of the 15th May, 1896:

"A feature of the annual report of the Protector of Immigrants, to which more public attention should be given than is the case, is that referring to the number of suicides which take place every year among the indentured coolies on the estates. This year the number recorded is six out of a total of 8,828. A large number occurred in 1894. It is, however, a very high percentage and raises the suspicion that on some estates a system of treatment exists towards the coolie labourers much akin to slave-driving. It is extremely significant that so many suicides should occur on certain estates. This is a point which calls for investigation. Apparently, no inquiry of any kind is held into the cases with a view to ascertain whether the treatment meted out to unfortunate wretches, who prefer death to life, is such as to render existence an intolerable misery. The matter is one which is apt to pass unnoticed. It, however, ought not to do so. In a recent case of desertion on the part of several coolies from an estate down South, the prisoners openly declared in Court that they would rather kill themselves than return to their employer. The Magistrate said he had no option but to order them back to serve out their indentures. It is time the Colony took steps to afford such complainants an opportunity of bringing the facts in connection with their complaints before some Court of Inquiry and the public. It is also desirable that a Secretary of Indian Affairs should be added to the Ministry. As matters stand at present, the indentured Indian has no effectual mode of appeal against whatever brutality may be inflicted on him on the plantations."

We, however, wish to guard ourselves against being understood to say that the life of the indentured Indians in Natal is harder than in any other country, or that this is a part of the general grievances of the Indians in the Colony. On the other hand, we know that there are estates in Natal where the Indians are very well treated. At the same time, we do humbly submit that the lot of the indentured Indians is not all that it might be and that there are points which require attention.

When an indentured Indian loses his free pass, he is charged ? for the duplicate. The reason for this is the alleged fraudulent sale by the Indians of their passes. But, surely, such fraudulent sale can be criminally punished. A man who has sold his pass should never be able to get a duplicate even on a payment of ?0. On the other hand, it should be as easy for an ordinary Indian to get a duplicate as the original. They are supposed to carry their passes about their persons. No wonder if they are frequently lost. I know a man who could not get a duplicate because he had not ? with him. He wanted to go to Johannesburg and he could not go. The practice in the Protector's department in such cases is to issue temporary passes so that the men may be able to make a present of their first ? earned to the Protector's office. In the case I am referring to, the man had a temporary pass issued for six months. He could not earn ? during that time. There are dozens of such cases. I have no hesitation in saying that this is nothing but a system of blackmail.

ZULULAND

In the Crown Colony of Zululand there are certain townships.

There are regulations published with reference to the sale of land in these townships, and the regulations for the townships of Eshowe and Nondweni prevent the Indians from owning or acquiring land although the Indians own land worth nearly ?,000 in the township of Melmoth in the same country. We have sent a memorial to Mr. Chamberlain and it is now engaging his attention. The Colonists in Natal say that, if such disabilities can be placed on Indians in a Crown Colony, a responsibly governed Colony such as Natal should be allowed to do what it liked with regard to the Indians. Our position in Zululand is no better than in the Free State. It is so dangerous to go to Zululand that the one or two who ventured to go there had to return back. There is a good opening for the Indians there, but the illtreatment comes in the way. This is a matter that we are earnestly hoping will be set right without much delay.

THE CAPE COLONY

In the Cape Colony, the Mayoral Congress has passed a resolution signifying its desire for legislation prohibiting the influx of Asiatics in that Colony and hoping that prompt action will be taken. The Cape Legislature has, lately, passed a measure which gives the East London Municipality in that Colony the power to make bye-laws compelling natives and Indians to remove to and reside in certain locations and prohibiting them from walking on foot-paths. It is difficult to conceive a better instance of cruel persecution. The following is the position of the Indians in East Griqualand under the Cape Government, according to the Mercury of 23rd March, 1896:

"An Arab, named Ismail Suliman, erected a store in East Griqualand, paid customs duty upon goods and applied for a licence, which the Magistrate refused. Mr. Attorney Francis, on the Arab's behalf, appealed to the Cape Government who upheld the Magistrate and have issued instructions that no coolies or Arabs are to have trading licences in East Griqualand and the one or two that have licences are to be closed up."

Thus, in some parts of Her Majesty's Dominions In South Africa, even the vested rights of her Indian subjects are not to be protected. What happened to the Indian in the end I was unable to ascertain. There are many cases where Indians have been unceremoniously refused licences to trade. There is a Bluebook on Native Affairs published in Natal. One of the Magistrates therein says he simply refuses to issue trading licences to Indians and thus prevents Indian encroachments.

CHARTERED TERRITORIES

In the Chartered Territories, the Indians are receiving the same kind of treatment. Only lately, an Indian was refused a licence to trade. He went to the Supreme Court who decided that the licence could not be refused to him. Now the Rhodesians have sent a petition to the Government requesting them to alter the law so as to prevent the Indians from getting licences under the request of the petitioners. This is what the correspondent of the South African Daily Telegraph has to say about the meeting that sent the petition:

"It affords me pleasure to be able to say, and say truthfully, that the meeting was in no way a representative one. Had it been so, little credit would thereby have been reflected on the inhabitants of the town. Some half a dozen leading storekeepers, the editor of a paper, a sprinkling of minor Government officials and a fairly large collection of prospectors, mechanics and artisans made up the assembly which those under whose direction it was held would have us believe represented the voice of the police of Salisbury. The resolutions, which I have already wired you with the [names of] proposers and seconders, were nicely cut and dried before the meeting commenced and the figures were set in order and worked in their places when the time arrived. There were no Indians present and no one ventured a word on their behalf. Why, it is hard to say, for it is certain that the feeling of by far the majority in this town is altogether adverse to the one-sided, selfish and narrow-minded opinion expressed by those who essayed to speak on the question... I cannot help thinking that little, if any, harm need be feared from the advent of a race who are industrious and steady and who, in higher sphere, have on occasion given evidences of their capabilities in upholding positions which they maintain ably and honourably side by side with their lighter-skinned brother."

THE TRANSVAAL

Coming now to the non-British States, i.e., the Transvaal and the Free State, there were in the Transvaal nearly two hundred traders in 1894 whose liquidated assets would amount to ?00,000. Of these, about three firms imported goods directly from England, Durban, Port Elizabeth, India and other places, and had thus branches in the other parts of the world whose existence mainly depended upon their Transvaal business. The rest were small vendors having stores in different places. There were,then, nearly two thousand hawkers in the Republic who buy goods and hawk them about. Of the labouring Indian population, who are employed as general servants in European houses or hotels, there were about 1,500 men, of whom about 1,000 lived in Johannesburg. Such, roughly, was the position at the end of 1894 A.D. The numbers have now considerably increased. In the Transvaal, the Indians cannot own landed property; they can be ordered to reside in locations. No new licences to trade are issued to them. They are made to pay a special registration fee of ?. All these restrictions are unlawful, being in contravention of the London Convention which secures the rights of all Her Majesty's subjects. But the previous Secretary of State for the Colonies having consented to a departure from the Convention, the Transvaal has been able to impose the above restrictions. They were the subject of an arbitration in 1894-95 which has decided against the Indians, that is to say, which has declared that the Republic was entitled to pass those laws. A memorial against the award of the arbitrator was sent to the Home Government. Mr. Chamberlain has now given his decision on the memorial and, while sympathizing with the prayer thereof, has accepted the award of the Arbitrator. He has, however, promised and retained the right to make friendly representations to the Transvaal Government from time to time. And, if the representations are emphatic enough, we have no doubt that we shall get justice in the end. We, therefore, implore the public bodies to exert their influence so that these representations may be such as to have their desired effect. I shall venture to quote an instance in point. When, during the Malaboch war, the British subjects were being commandeered, many protested against it and asked for the interference of the Home Government. The reply first sent was to the effect that they could not interfere with the affairs of the Republic. The papers, however, were enraged and memorials strongly worded were repeated. At last came the request to the Transvaal Government not to commandeer British subjects. It was not an interference, yet the request had to be granted and the commandeering of British subjects was stopped. May we hope for such a request which carries with it its fulfilment? If we are not as important a community as that concerned with the commando movement our grievances, we submit, are much more so. Whether such or any representations are made or not, there will arise questions out of the award that will engage Mr. Chamberlain's attention.

What shall be done with the hundreds of Indian stores in the Transvaal? Will they all be closed up? Will they all be made to live in locations, and if so, what locations? The British Agent has thus described the Transvaal locations with reference to the removal of the Malays in Pretoria, the metropolis of the South African Republic:

To be forced into a small location on a spot used as a place to deposit the refuse of the town, without any water except the polluted soakage in the gully between the location and the town, must inevitably result in malignant fevers and other diseases breaking out amongst them whereby their lives and the health of the community in town will be endangered. (Green book No. 2, 1893, page 72)

Will they or will they not receive any compensation if they are made to sell off? Again, the very law is ambiguous. The Arbitrator was called upon to decide upon the interpretation which he has now left to the High Court of the Transvaal. We contend that by the law the State can only compel us to reside in locations. The State contends that residence includes trading stores also and that, therefore, we may not, under that law, even trade except in specified locations. The High court is said to favour the State interpretation.

Nor are these the only grievances in the Transvaal. These were the subject of the arbitration. But there is a law which prevents the railway authorities in the Transvaal from issuing first or second-class tickets on the railways. There is a tin compartment reserved for natives and other coloured people in which we are literally packed like sheep, without regard to our dress, our behaviour or our position. In Natal, there is no such law but the petty officials give trouble. The hardship is not insignificant. In Delagoa Bay, the authorities so respect the Indian that they would not allow him to travel 3rd class, so much so that, if a poor Indian could not afford the 2nd-class fare, he is allowed to travel 2nd class under a 3rd-class ticket. The same Indian, as soon as he reaches the Transvaal border, is compelled to put his dignity into his pocket, asked to produce a pass and then unceremoniously thrust into the third-class compartment, no matter whether he has a first-class or a second-class ticket.

The journey is long enough to be felt like a month's journey in those uncomfortable quarters. The same thing happens on the Natal side. Four months ago, an Indian gentleman got a second-class ticket for Pretoria at Durban. He was assured that he would be all right, yet he was not only forcibly put out at Volksrust, a station on the Transvaal border, but could not proceed by that train because it did not carry any third-class compartment. These regulations seriously interfere with our carrying on our trade also. There are many who, owing to such inconveniences, would not move from place to place unless they could not possibly avoid it.

Then, in the Transvaal, an Indian, like the native of South Africa, has to carry a travelling pass which costs a shilling. This is the Indian's permit to travel about. It is, I believe, available only for a single journey. Thus, Mr. Haji Mahomed Haji Dada was put out of his post-cart and had to walk a distance of three miles, at the point of the policeman's sjambok, which serves the purpose of the bayonet, in order to get the pass. The pass master, however, knew him and so would not issue any pass to him. All the same, he had to miss his coach and walk from Volksrust to Charlestown.

The Indians cannot, as of right, walk on the foot-path in Pretoria and Johannesburg. I use the word "as of right" advisedly, because the traders are, as a rule, not interfered with. In Johannesburg, there is a bye-law to that effect passed by the Sanitary Board. A gentleman, named Mr. Pillay, a graduate of the Madras University, was violently pushed off the foot-path in Pretoria. He wrote about it to the papers. The attention of the British Agent also was drawn to the matter. But, sympathetic as he was towards the Indians, he declined to interfere.

The gold-mining laws of Johannesburg prevent Indians from taking out mining licences and render it criminal for them to sell or possess native gold.

The treaty, exempting the British subjects from commando service, has been accepted by the Transvaal with the reservation that British subjects therein shall mean only "whites". That is now the subject of a memorial to Mr.

Chamberlain. Under it, apart from the serious disability it places upon the Indian subjects of Her Majesty, we might, as the London Times puts it, "now see a levy of British Indian subjects driven at the point of the Transvaal bayonets against the bayonets of British Troops".

THE ORANGE FREE STATE

The Orange Free State, as I have already quoted from a newspaper, has made the British Indian an impossibility. We are driven away from that State causing to us a loss of ?,000. Our stores were closed up and no compensation was given to us. Will Mr. Chamberlain consider this a real grievance and get us our ?,000 from the Orange Free State, not to speak of the future blighting of the prospects of the traders particularly concerned? I know them all, and most of them have not been able to regain their former position, although at the time they were thus driven out they were supposed to be the wealthiest firms. The law, which is entitled "the law to prevent the inrush of Asiatic coloured persons", prevents any Indian from remaining in the Orange Free State for more than 2 months, unless he gets the permission from the President of the Republic who cannot consider the application to reside before thirty days have elapsed after the presentation of the petition and other ceremonies have been performed. He can, however, on no account, hold fixed property in the State or carry on any mercantile or farming business.

The President may or may not, "according to the state of things", grant such mutilated permission to reside. Any Indian resident, moreover, is subject to an annual poll-tax of ?0. The first contravention of the section relating to mercantile and farming business renders the delinquent liable to a fine of ?5 or three months' imprisonment, with or without hard labour. For all subsequent contraventions, the punishment is to be doubled.

Such then is the position of the Indians in South Africa, except Delagoa Bay where the Indians are very much respected, labour under no special disability and are owners of nearly half the fixed property in the principal streets of that city. They are all of them mostly traders. Some of them are in Government employment also. There are two Parsee gentlemen who are Engineers. And there is another Parsee gentleman whom, perhaps, even a child in Delagoa Bay knows by the name of "Senhor Edul". The trading class, however, chiefly consists of Mahomedans and Banias, mostly from Portuguese India.

It yet remains for me to examine the cause of this deplorable state of things, as also the remedy. The Europeans say that the habits of the Indians are insanitary, they spend nothing and that they are untruthful and immoral. These are the objections according to the most moderate journals. Others, of course, simply abuse us. The charge as to insanitary habits and untruthfulness is partially true, that is to say, the sanitary habits of the Indian community as a whole, in South Africa, are not as good as they might be from the highest point of view. The charge as laid against us by the European community and used in the way it has been, we totally deny, and we have quoted the opinions of doctors in South Africa to show that "class considered, the lowest-class Indian lives better and in better habitation and with more regard to sanitary measures than the lowest-class white". Dr. Veale, B.A., M.B.B.S. (Cantab.), finds the Indians "to be cleanly in their persons and free from the personal diseases due to dirt or careless habits" and finds also that "their dwellings are generally clean and sanitation is willingly attended to by them." But we do not say we are beyond improvement in this matter. We may not live quite satisfactorily if there were no sanitary laws. Both the communities err equally in this respect, as the newspaper records would show. That, however, cannot be a reason for all the serious disabilities that are imposed upon us. The cause lies elsewhere, as I shall presently show. Let them enforce the sanitary law very strictly, and we shall be all the better for that. Those of us who are lazy will be properly aroused from our lethargy. As to untruthfulness, the charge, to a certain extent, is true, with regard to the indentured Indians, utterly exaggerated with regard to the traders. But the indentured Indians, placed in the position they are, I venture to say, have done much better than any other community would do in a similar position. The very fact that they are liked as servants by the Colonists and called "useful and trusty", shows that they are not the incorrigible liars they are made out to be. However, the moment they leave India, they are free from the healthy checks that keep them on the narrow path. In South Africa, they are without any religious instruction, though they need it badly. They are called upon to give evidence against their masters for the sake of a fellow brother. This duty they often shirk. Gradually, therefore, their faculty for adhering to the truth, under all circumstances, becomes perverted and they become helpless afterwards.

I submit that they are more the objects of pity than of contempt. And this view I ventured to place before the public in South Africa two years ago, and they have not excepted to it. The fact that the European firms in South Africa give hundreds of Indians large credit practically on their word of honour, and have no cause to regret having done so, and that the banks give Indians almost unlimited credit, while the merchants and bankers would not trust Europeans to that extent, conclusively prove that the Indian traders cannot be so dishonest as they are made out to be. I do not, of course, mean to convey that the European firms believe the Indians to be more truthful than the Europeans. But I do humbly think that, while they would perhaps trust both equally, they rely upon the Indian's thrift, his determination not to ruin his creditor and his temperate habits. A bank has been giving credit to an Indian to a very large extent. A European gentleman, known to the bank and a friend of this Indian, wanted ?00 credit for speculation. The bank refused to give him credit without guarantee. The Indian friend pledged his honour, and that was all he had to pledge, and the bank accepted that security, although at the time, too, he was heavily in debt to the bank. The result is the European friend has failed to refund the ?00 to the bank, and the Indian friend, for the present, has lost the money. The European, of course, lives in a better style and requires some drink for his dinners, and our Indian friend drinks only water. The charges that we spend nothing and are immoral, i.e., more than those who bring the charges against us, we repudiate entirely. But the real cause is the trade jealousy, in the first instance, and want of knowledge about Indian and the Indians, in the second.

The hue and cry against the Indians was first raised by the traders and then taken up by the populace till, at last, the prejudice permeated the high and the low. This can be seen from the South African legislation affecting Indians. The Orange Free Staters have frankly stated that they hate the Asiatic because he is a successful trader. The Chambers of Commerce in the different States were the first movers. And they, of course, came out with the statements that we believed the Christians a natural prey, and that we believed our women to be soulless and were propagators of leprosy and syphilis and other diseases. The matters have now reached such a stage that for a good Christian gentleman it is as natural to see nothing unjust in the persecution of the Asiatic as it was in the olden days for the bonafide Christians to see nothing wrong or un-Christian in slavery. Mr. Henry Bale is a legislator in the Natal Assembly, a typical English gentleman, and is dubbed Bale the Conscientious because he is a converted Christian and takes a prominent part in religious movements and brings his conscience often into play on the floor of the Assembly House. Yet, this gentleman is one of the most powerful and uncompromising opponents of Indians, and gives his certificate that an annual poll-tax of ? on a body of men who have been the mainstay of the Colony, and compulsory return of such men, are just and humane measures.

Our method in South Africa is to conquer this hatred by love. At any rate, that is our goal. We would often fall short of that ideal but we can adduce innumerable instances to show that we have acted in that spirit. We do not attempt to have individuals punished but as a rule, patiently suffer wrongs at their hands. Generally, our prayers are not to demand compensation for past injuries, but to render a repetition of those injuries impossible and to remove the causes. Our grievances have been laid before the Indian public in the same spirit. If we have quoted instances of personal injuries, that we have done not for the purpose of seeking compensation but for that of laying our position vividly before the public in India. We are trying to remove any causes that may be in us for such treatment. But we cannot succeed without the sympathy and support of the public men in India, and without strong representations from the Home and Indian Governments. The want of knowledge about India is so great in South Africa that the people would not even believe us if we said that India is not dotted by huts only. The work done on our behalf by the London Times, the British Committee of the Congress and by Mr. Bhownaggree and in India by The Times of India, has borne fruit already. Of course, the question of the position of the Indians has been treated as an Imperial question, and almost every statesman whom we have approached has expressed his full sympathy to us. We have letters of sympathy from both the Conservative and Liberal members of the House of Commons. The Daily Telegraph has also extended its support to us. When the Franchise Bill was first passed and there was some talk of its disallowance, the public men and the newspapers in Natal said the Bill would be passed over and over again till Her Majesty's Government were tired. They rejected the British subject "humbug", and one paper went so far as to say that they would throw over their allegiance to the Queen if the Bill was disallowed. The Ministers openly declared that they would decline to govern the Colony if the Bill was disallowed. This was the time when the writer of the "Colonial Affairs" in the London Times favoured the Natal Bill. But the Thunderer, when it dealt with the matter, specially changed its tone. The Colonial Secretary seemed to be decisive and the despatch with reference to the Transvaal Arbitration arrived in time. This changed the whole tone of the Press in Natal. They protested but they were a part and parcel of the British Empire. The Natal Advertiser, which at one time proposed the formation of an anti-Asiatic League, thus dealt with the Indian question in a leading article, dated the 28th February, 1895. After alluding to the then reported disallowance of the Franchise Bill and the resolution of the Mayoral Congress in the Cape Colony before referred to, the article goes on:

"The problem, therefore, when looked at as a whole from the imperial to the purely local standpoint, is a very large and complex one. But however prone localities may be to regard the subject simply from the local stanpoint, it should be apparent to all who wish to study the matter in all its bearings (the only way in which a sound and healthy judgment can be arrived at), that the wider or Imperial considerations must also be taken into account. And further, as regards the purely local aspect of the case, it is quite as necessary, and perhaps as difficult, to discover whether a comprehensive view of the position is being taken or whether imperfect opinions are being formed on one side or the other through the acceptance of only such data as prejudice or self-interest may find acceptable. The general opinion existing throughout South Africa, as regards Indian emigration, may be summed up in the words, "We don't want them".

"The first point to be weighed is this that, in belonging to the British Empire, we have to take whatever may be evil as well as whatever may be good as arising from that connection, provided, of course, it is inseparable therefrom. Now, as regards the destinies of India's population, it may be taken for granted that the Imperial Government will not readily permit of legislation in any British dependency which has for its avowed object the repulsion of India's surplus population from any part of the British dominions; or, to put it the other way, which embodies the principle, so far as the particular legislating State is concerned, that India's teeming and fast increasing millions must be confined, and ultimately smothered, within India itself. On the contrary, the desire of the British Government is to remove from India the possibilities of such congestion, and to thereby render it a prosperous and happy, instead of a dangerous and discontented, portion of the British Empire. If India is to be retained as an advantageous part of the Empire, then it is absolutely necessary that means shall be found for relieving it of much of its present population, and it may be taken to be a part of the Imperial policy that India's surplus population is to be encouraged, rather than discouraged, to find fresh outlets in those other portions of the Empire which are in need of a labouring population. It will thus be seen that the question of coolie immigration into the British Colonies is one which reaches down to the deepest amelioration and salvation of India; it may even mean the inclusion or exclusion of that great possession in or from the British Empire. That is the Imperial aspect of the question, and is one which points directly to a desire on the part of the Imperial Government to do all in its power to prevent the raising, in other portions of the Empire, of barriers for the prevention of Indian immigration.

"As regards the local aspect of Indian immigration, what has to be considered is whether and if so, how far, does this Imperial policy conflict with what is desirable for this particular locality? There are those who absolutely condemn Indian immigration into this Colony, but it is doubtful whether these have given full consideration on all the bearings of the case. In the first place, those who so oppose Indian immigration have to answer the question: What would this Colony have done without them in those departments of industry in which they have undoubtedly proved useful? There is unquestionably much that is undesirable about the coolie, but before his presence here is condemned as an unmixed evil, it has to be shown that the Colony would have been better without him. This, we think, would be somewhat difficult to prove. There can be no question that the coolie is the best fitted, under existing local conditions, for the field labour required in connection with the agriculture of the Colony. Such work can never be undertaken in this climate by white men; our natives show little disposition or aptitude for it. This being so, who is ousted by the presence of the coolie as an agricultural labourer? No one. The work had either to be done by him or left undone altogether. Again, the coolie is largely employed by Government especially on the railway. What is the objection to him there? It may be said he is taking the place of the white man there; but is he? There may be a few isolated cases in which this contention could afford to replace all the Indians employed in the Government service by white men. Further, the towns in Natal are almost entirely dependent for their supply of vegetables upon the coolies, who farm plots of ground in the vicinity. With whom does the coolie interfere in this direction? Certainly not with the white man. Our farmers, as a body, have not yet acquired a taste for kitchen gardening sufficient to keep the market fully supplied. Neither does he interfere with the native, who, being the incarnation of indolence, does not, as a rule, trouble about the cultivation of anything except mealies for himself. Our own natives ought to have been our labouring class, but the fact has to be faced that, in this respect, they are almost a dead failure. Consequently, coloured labour of a more active and reliable kind had to be procured from some other source, and India has offered the necessary supply. The debt which the white man owes to these coloured labourers is this that they, by occupying the lowest stratum of society in those mixed communities of which they form a part, raise the white man one stratum higher right through the social scale than he otherwise would have occupied, had the menial offices been discharged by a European class. For instance, the white man, who is 'boss' over a gang of coolies, would have had himself to form one of the gang of labourers, had there been no black labourer.

"Again, the man who, in Europe, would have been that man's foreman, in this country develops into a master tradesman. And as in every other direction, by the presence of a black labouring class, the whites are set free to throw their efforts into higher planes than they could have done, had the majority of them had to devote their lives to the arduous labours of toilers of the lowest order. It will, therefore, probably yet be found that the removal of the drawbacks, at present incidental to the immigration of Indians into British Colonies, is not to be effected so much by the adoption of an obsolete policy of exclusion as by an enlightened and progressive application of ameliorating laws to those Indians who settle in them. One of the chief objections to Indians in that they do not live in accordance with European rules. The remedy for this is to gradually raise their mode of life by compelling them to live in better dwellings and by creating among them new wants, it will probably be found easier, because more in accord with the great onward movement of mankind, to demand to such settlers that they shall rise to their new conditions, than to endeavour to maintain the status quo ante by their entire exclusion."

Such articles (and they can be quoted by the dozen from the various newspapers) show that application of sufficient pressure from the Home Government can bring about a healthy change in the Indian policy of the Colonies, and that, even in the worst places, British love of justice and fair play can be roused. These two are the sheet-anchor of our hope. No amount of spreading information about India on our part can do any good without the much-needed application of the pressure.

The following article, from the pen of a veteran journalist in South Africa, shows also that there are men in South Africa who would rise above their surroundings and disclose the true British character:

It sometimes happens in life that men are called upon to decide decisively between the claims of justice and the claims of self. With men of honourable inclination, the task is, of course, a far heavier one than with men whose natures have long ago cast overboard any conscientious scruples with which they may have been endowed at the outset of their unlovely existence. From men who will puff rotten companies at the very moment they are selling out and individuals of a like character, it is, of course, perfectly absurd to expect any other result than that self will predominate, but with the average commercial man, justice is more often the victor in the ethical conflict. Amongst the causes of these conflicts, as they affect South Africans generally and British Transvaalers in particular, is the question of the 'coolie traders', as our Indian and Arab fellow citizens are designated. It is the position of these merchants, for so they really are, which has aroused so much attention and which is still productive of no little interest and hostility to this day. And it is in considering their position that their rivals in trade have sought to inflict upon them, through the medium of the State, what looks, on the face of it, something very like an injustice for the benefit of self.

The outcry which was raised in the capital of the Transvaal against the coolie trader some little time ago is brought to the mind by occasional paragraphs in the morning papers regarding the doings of the Indian and Arab dealers.

In the face of such reminders as these, one may reasonably expect to be pardoned for referring, for a few moments, to a body of respectable, hard-working men, whose position is so misunderstood that their very nationality is overlooked, and a name labelled to them which tends to place them on an exceedingly low level in the estimation of their fellow creatures.

In the face, too, of financial operations, the success of which many of their detractors would envy one fails to understand the agitation which would place the operators in the same category as the half-heathen native and confine them to locations and subject them to the harsher laws by which the Transvaal Kaffir is governed. The impression, which is but too prevalent both in the Transvaal and this Colony, that the quiet and altogether inoffensive 'Arab' shopkeeper, and the equally harmless Indian, who carries his pack of dainty wares from house to house, is a 'coolie', is due largely to an indolent ignorance as to the race whence they sprang. When one reflects that the conception of Brahminism, with its poetic and mysterious mythology, took its rise in the land of the 'coolie trader', that in that land, twenty-four centuries ago, the almost divine Buddha taught and practised the glorious doctrine of self-sacrifice, and that it was from the plains and mountains of that weird old country that are derived the fundamental truths of the very language we speak, one cannot but help regretting that the children of such a race should be treated as the equals of the children of black heathendom and outer darkness. Those who, for a few moments, have stayed to converse with the Indian trader have been, perhaps, surprised to find they are speaking to a scholar and a gentleman. In the schools of Bombay, Madras, and even from under the very shadows of the Himalayas and from the plains of the Punjab, these unassuming individuals have drunk deep the springs of knowledge, it may be, unsuited to our requirements, foreign to our taste, and savouring too much of the mythical to be of use in our practical lives, but, nevertheless, a knowledge the acquisition of which requires as much application, as much literary application, and a far more sensitive and poetic nature than is required in the highest schools of Oxford or Cambridge. The philosophy of India, obscured by the dust of ages and the traditions of generations, was taught with delight, when the ancestors of the Superior Boer and the Superior Englishman were content to find their highest pleasures in the pursuit of the bear and the wolf over the marshes and through the forests of their native lands. When these same ancestors has had no thought of a higher life, when selfpreservation was their first law, and the destruction of their neighbour's village and the capture of his wife and infant their keenest enjoyment, the philosophers of India had grown weary with a thousand years' conflict with the problems of existence. And it is the sons of this land of light who are despised as coolies and treated as Kaffirs.

It is about time that those who cry out against the Indian merchant should have pointed out to them who and what he is. Many of his worst detractors are British subjects enjoying all the privileges and rights of membership in a glorious community. To them the hatred of injustice and the love of fair play is inherent, and when it affects themselves, they have a method of insisting upon their rights and liberties, whether under a foreign government or under their own. Possibly, it has never struck them that the Indian merchant is also a British subject and claims the same liberties and rights with equal justice. To say the very least of it, if we may be permitted to employ a phrase of Palmerston's days, it is very un-English to claim rights one would not allow to others. The right of trade as an equal privilege has, since the abolition of the Elizabethan monopolies, become almost a part of the English Constitution, and were anyone to interfere with that right, the privilege of British citizenship would very suddenly come to the front. Because the Indian is more successful in competition and lives on less than the English merchant, is the unfairest and weakest of arguments. The very foundation of English commerce lies in the fact of our being able to compete more successfully with other nations. Surely, it is Protection running to madness when English traders wish the State to intervene to protect them against the more successful operations of their rivals. The injustice to the Indians is so glaring that one is almost ashamed of one's countrymen in wishing to have these men treated as natives, simply because of their success in trade. The very reason that they have been so successful against the dominant race is sufficient to raise them above that degrading level. (Cape Times, 13-4-1889)

The question resolves itself into this: "May the British Indians when they leave India," in the words of the London Times, "have the same status before the law as other British subjects enjoy? May they or may they not go freely from one British possession to another and claim the rights of British subjects in allied States?" Says the same journal again:

"The Indian Government and the Indians themselves believe that it is in Southern Africa that this question of their status must be determined. If they secure the position of British subjects in South Africa, it will be almost impossible to deny it to them elsewhere. If they fail to secure that position in South Africa, it will be extremely difficult for them to attain it elsewhere."

Thus, then, the decision of the question will affect not only the Indians at present settled in South Africa but the whole future emigration of Indians and, also, the position of Indian immigrants in other parts of Her Majesty's Dominions and allied States. In Australia they are endeavouring to pass laws to restrict, the influx of Indians in those parts. Temporary and local relief, while absolutely necessary for the cases now before the two Governments for consideration, will be of no avail, unless the whole question is decided once for all, for "the whole body is rotten and not parts only". Mr. Bhownaggree has questioned Mr. Chamberlain "whether he will take immediate steps to arrest legislation of this description by the Government of Natal and other parts of Her Majesty's Dominions in Africa". There may yet be laws and regulations besides what have been alluded to herein and which may not be known to us. Unless, therefore, all such past legislation is declared illegal and further legislation stopped, we have a very dismal outlook before us, for the struggle is unequal, and how long are we to go on troubling the Colonial Office and the Indian Government? The Times of India has been our advocate when we were almost without any. The British Committee of the Congress has always worked on our behalf. The powerful aid of the London Times has, by itself, raised us a step higher in the estimation of the South Africans. Mr. Bhownaggree has been incessant in his efforts on our behalf ever since he entered Parliament. We know we have the sympathy of the public bodies in India, but our object in laying our grievances specially before the Indian public is to enlist the very active sympathy of all the public bodies in India. That is my commission, and our cause is so great and just that I have no doubt I shall return to Natal with satisfactory result.

M. K. GANDHI

PS. -- If any gentleman is anxious to study further the Indian question in South Africa and requires the various memorials referred to herein, an effort will be made to supply him with copies of the same.

M. K. GANDHI